More Tunes for Ten Fingers

A second piano book for young beginners

by

Pauline Hall

Illustrations by Caroline Crossland

Reprinted with corrections 1993. This Edition 2015

Welcome to your new book!

There are lots of new tunes for you to play, and new notes to learn.

Don't forget — the more you play, the better your playing will become, and the more you'll enjoy it.

Keep your hand in a nice bridge-shape as you play, with your fingers on their tips.

Could a mouse sit under your bridge?

In these boxes are things that you know already, but just check, to make sure that you do.

Row, row, row your boat

You can play this tune on its own, or with a duet part. It should sound lovely and smooth.

Row,   row,   row   your   boat   gen - tly   down   the   stream,_____

mer - ri - ly,   mer - ri - ly,   mer - ri - ly,   mer - ri - ly,   life   is   but   a   dream._____

Duet part

Rests

Do you remember about rests?

A rest is a silence.

Every note has its own rest sign.

This is a ♩ rest:

This is a ♩ rest:

(like a little black brick sitting on the third line).

This is a o rest:

(it is also a whole-bar rest).

It hangs down from the fourth line.

In the next tunes say '*ssh!*' on all the rests.

In our house (*ssh!*) there's a mouse, (*ssh, ssh!*) so neat on sound - less feet. (*ssh!*)

Cuck - oo!   (*ssh, ssh, ssh!*) cuck - oo! (*ssh!*)

Here's a trick to catch you out! Play this tune.

What did it sound like?

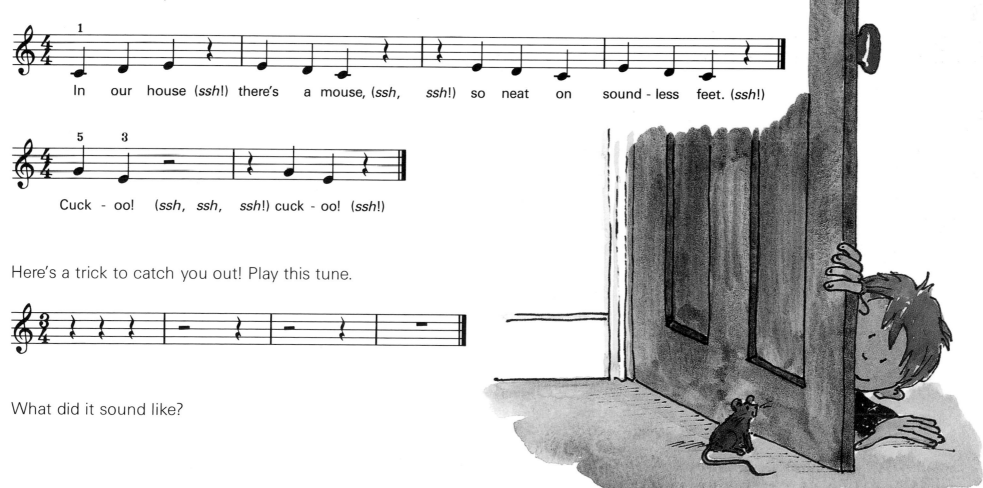

We Three Kings

The Skaters

Play this as smoothly as you can. Your right hand is the first skater; it's joined by its partner, and then they skate together.

Gracefully

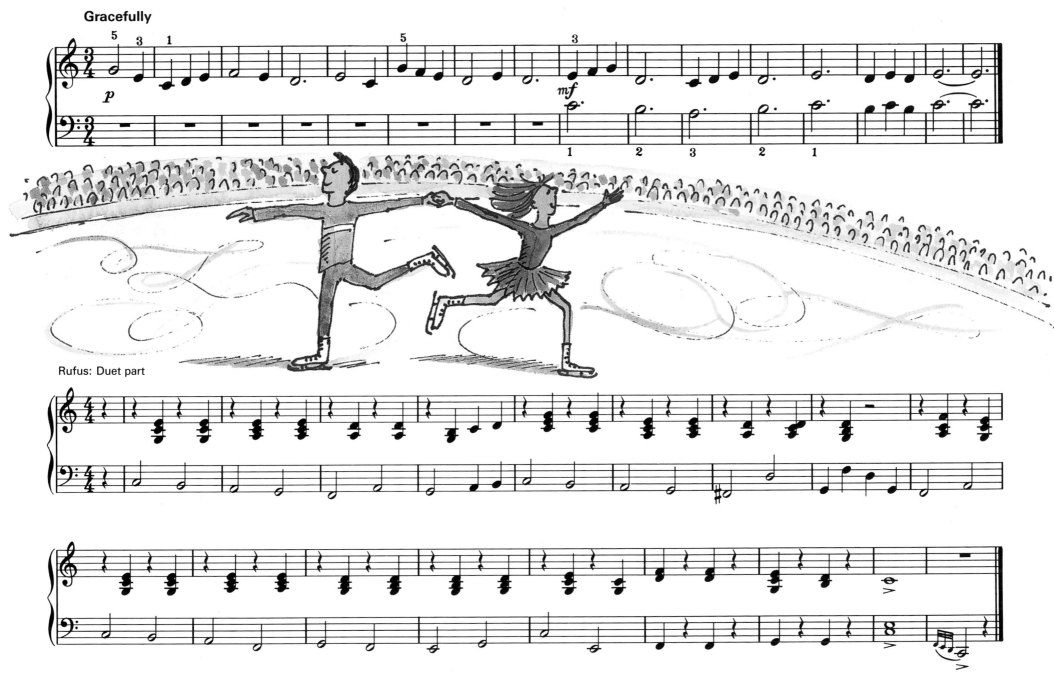

Rufus: Duet part

8va bassa

Rufus

If you want to play this as a duet, you should play your part one octave higher. The duet part is on the facing page.

I know a dog called Ru - fus who dreams while he's a-sleep.   He thinks he's cha-sing rab-bits,   or round-ing up the sheep.   He

wuf-fles and he snuf-fles, and scrab-bles with his paws,   And scat-ters all the rab-bits with his loud   fer - o - cious   snores!

Staccato

A dot over or under a note like this 𝅘𝅥 or this 𝅘𝅥 makes the note short and jumpy.
Choose any note and play this with your 3rd finger. Make it bounce, and don't forget the rests.

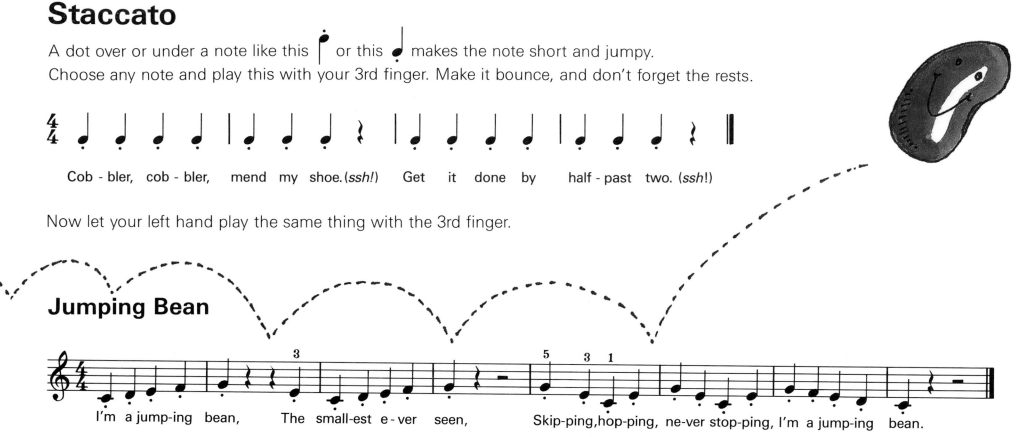

Cob - bler, cob - bler, mend my shoe. *(ssh!)* Get it done by half - past two. *(ssh!)*

Now let your left hand play the same thing with the 3rd finger.

Jumping Bean

I'm a jump-ing bean, The small-est e - ver seen, Skip-ping, hop-ping, ne-ver stop-ping, I'm a jump-ing bean.

You could try playing this starting on the highest C on the piano. Then it really would sound like a very small bean.

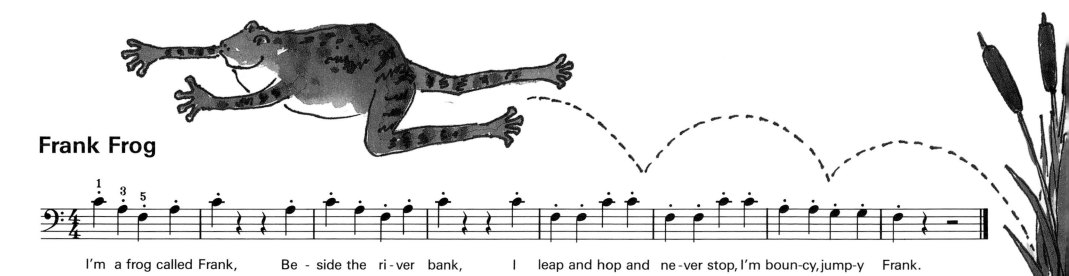

Frank Frog

I'm a frog called Frank, Be - side the ri - ver bank, I leap and hop and ne - ver stop, I'm boun-cy, jump-y Frank.

Legato

This means that the sounds are smooth and joined up.
Sometimes the notes are grouped under a curved line:
They look as if they are under an umbrella.

Walk your fingers smoothly up and down these notes.

Walk-ing up and down a - gain to C.

Try it with your left hand, starting with your 5th finger.

Smooth Snake

Sam's a smooth and slip-pery snake, Li-ving down be - side the lake, Smooth-ly gli-ding, sli-ther - sli-ding, Sam's a slip-pery snake.

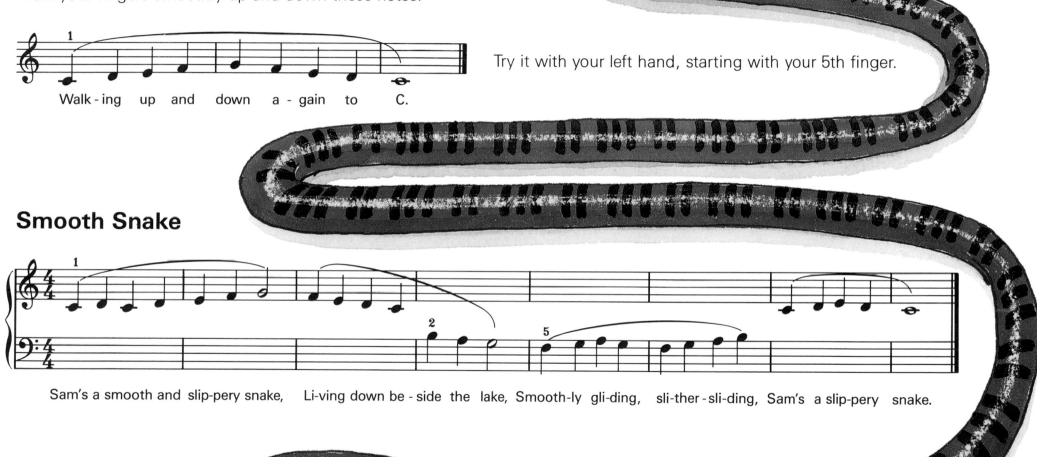
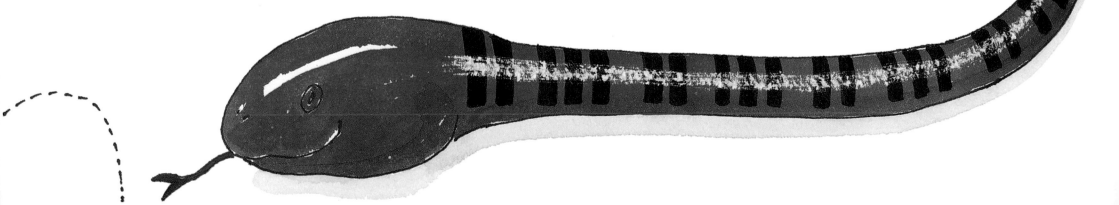

Black keys

Would you like to play some black keys? Right!

This is a **sharp** sign: ♯ (a bit like noughts and crosses).

When it sits in front of a note, you must play the next-door note UP to the *right* (it's usually a black key).

This is F sharp (F♯)

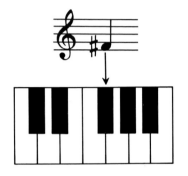

Play all the F♯s on the piano.

See how quickly you can find these notes: F♯ B C♯ D A G♯.

Up and Down the Ladder

Duet part

Look and play

Look at each tune carefully, and put your fingers over the right keys.

Then see if you can play the tune WITHOUT LOOKING AT YOUR HANDS!

Don't worry — your fingers know what to do.

Count steadily as you play.

Here's a really difficult one! Get your fingers ready — then go!

Another tricky one for your left hand.

Carillon

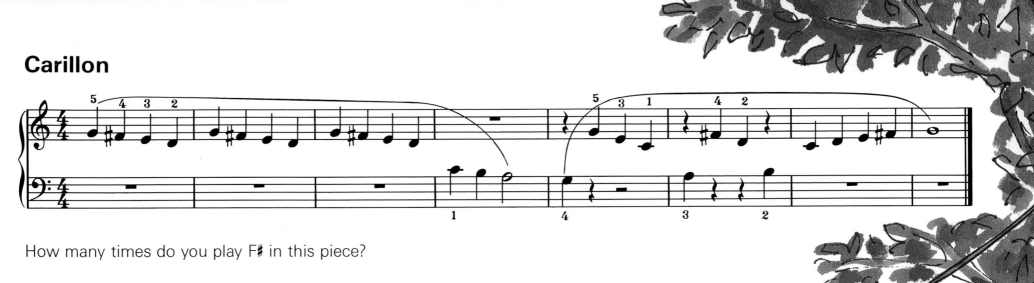

How many times do you play F# in this piece?

You could try holding the right pedal down throughout this piece, to make it sound really bell-like.

♮ This sign is called a **natural**.
It means the ordinary note — not a sharp (or flat).
Look out for one in *Swing Song*.

Swing Song

Very smoothly

Duet part

Why don't you try playing *Swing Song* through twice, the first time on your own and the second time with the duet part?

A Puzzle Page

Write a 𝅝 on every line.
How many did you write?

Write a 𝅝 in every space.
How many did you write?

Here are some balloons. Can you draw a string from each one to its own number of counts?

Draw a ☐ round each note on a line.
Draw a ○ round each note in a space.

Draw some treble clefs

and some bass clefs.

Some long names

o (4 counts) is called a **semibreve.**

♩ (2 counts) is called a **minim.**

♩. (3 counts) is called a **dotted minim.**

♩ (1 count) is called a **crotchet.**

♪ ($\frac{1}{2}$ count) is called a **quaver.**

Draw each note beside its name.

minim

semibreve

crotchet

quaver

dotted minim

When two quavers are written together, they are like twins and join hands like this:

Sometimes two sets of twins join up like this:

Fun with quavers

You don't need a piano for this.
You can either close the piano lid, or use a table.
When you come to a rest, give a sniff!
Follow the dotted lines.

Jungle Drums

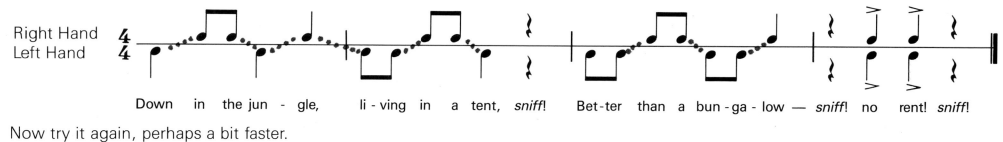

Down   in   the jun - gle,   li - ving   in   a   tent, *sniff*!   Bet-ter   than   a   bun - ga - low — *sniff*!   no   rent! *sniff*!

Now try it again, perhaps a bit faster.

Coming round the Mountain

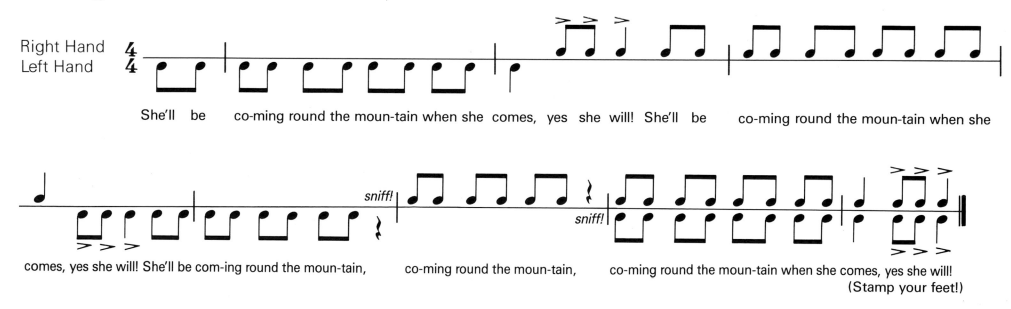

She'll   be   co-ming round the moun-tain when she comes, yes she will! She'll be   co-ming round the moun-tain when she

comes, yes she will! She'll be com-ing round the moun-tain,   co-ming round the moun-tain,   co-ming round the moun-tain when she comes, yes she will!
(Stamp your feet!)

>>These little signs are **accents**. They tell you to play their notes more firmly.

To the rescue

There is a mixture of crotchets  and quavers in this tune. Keep the quavers steady, and fit them in exactly to a crotchet count.

My lit-tle bro-ther's name is Sam, he's ve-ry fond of bugs; he has a shi-ny cen-ti-pede, a bee-tle, and two slugs. He

keeps them in the gar-den shed and feeds them ev-ery day; I'm going to o-pen up their box, and let them run a-way!

There are only two counts in the last bar, because you started with an odd one at the beginning.

I'd like to be a Tea-bag

I'd like to be a tea-bag, and stay at home all day, And talk to o-ther tea-bags in a tea-bag sort of

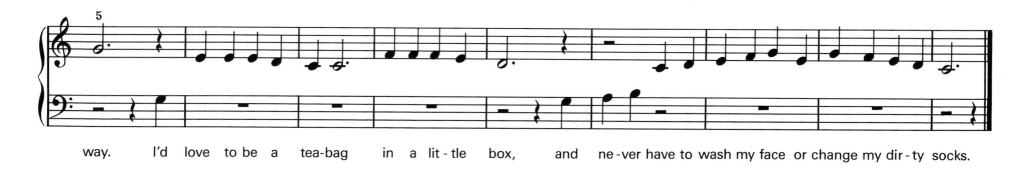

way. I'd love to be a tea-bag in a lit-tle box, and ne-ver have to wash my face or change my dir-ty socks.

Words from the poem 'Teabag' by Peter Dixon (*Grow Your Own Poems*, Macmillan Education, 1991).

A voyage of discovery

Your left hand ventures into new territory.
These are the notes you know already.

Play this little tune to make sure.

With your 2nd finger, hop down these five notes and add three more.

E D C

New notes

You have always played F and G with your 4th and 5th fingers.
Now try using your 1st and 2nd.

Play your new notes with these fingers:

5 4 3 2 1

Try this exercise for your 5th, 4th, and 3rd fingers.

5   4 3 4   5   4 3 4

Walk - ing up and straight a - long,   Walk - ing makes my fin - gers strong.

Low C   Low D   Low E
in a space on a line   in a space

Some tunes for your left hand in new territory

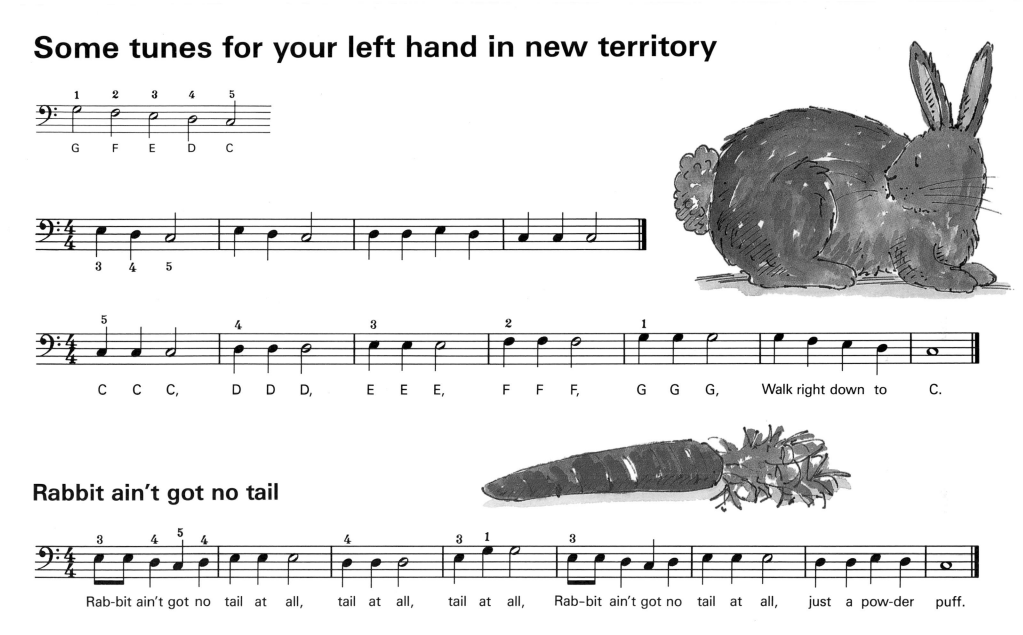

G F E D C

C C C, D D D, E E E, F F F, G G G, Walk right down to C.

Rabbit ain't got no tail

Rab-bit ain't got no tail at all, tail at all, tail at all, Rab-bit ain't got no tail at all, just a pow-der puff.

Go and tell Aunt Dinah

Sadly

Go and tell Aunt Di - nah, go and tell Aunt Din - ah, go and tell Aunt Di - nah, the old grey goose is dead.

Musical Houses

All these people are lost.
Can you put them in their musical houses by tapping their names and matching them to the right house?
Then write the number of their house beside their names.

Hairdresser
Lorry-driver
Dentist
Sergeant-major
Vet
Milkman
Carpenter
Pop-singer
Nurse
Bus-conductor
Rat-catcher
Engineer
Butcher
Fisherman

Which house would these people feel at home in?

Robin Hood
Old MacDonald
Jack Sprat
Sherlock Holmes
Batman
Cinderella
Peter Pan

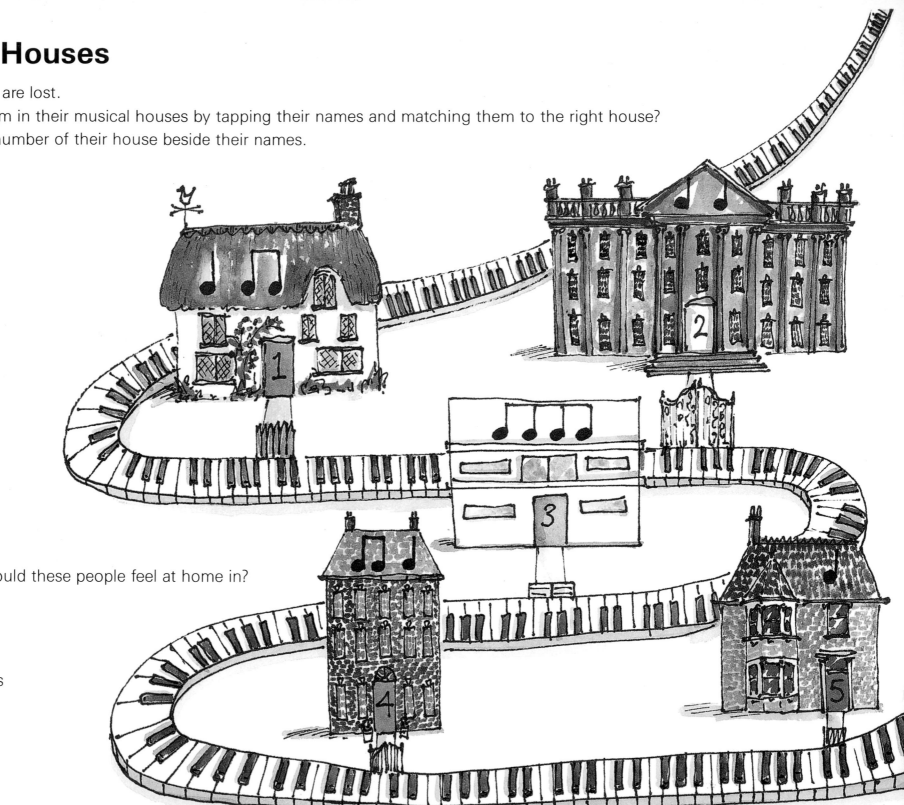

Steps and skips

When you play next-door notes, use next-door fingers like this:

When you miss a note and there is a gap, miss out a finger like this:

Now let your left hand try. In this tune there is a mixture of steps and skips.

The Lonely Piper

This is the chance to make your playing sound like bag-pipes!

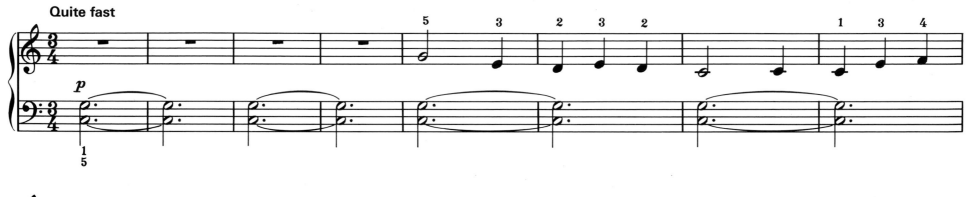

More black keys

This is a **flat** sign: ♭. When it sits in front of a note, you play the next note DOWN to the *left* (it's usually a black key).

This is E flat (E♭).

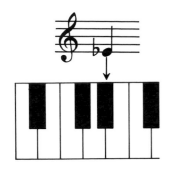

Find these notes, quick as you can!: C E flat G B♭ D A♭.

Can you spot the flat in the next tune? It comes twice.

Russian Song

When your fingers know this tune, you can play it fast.

Chords

When two or more notes are played together, they are called a **chord**.

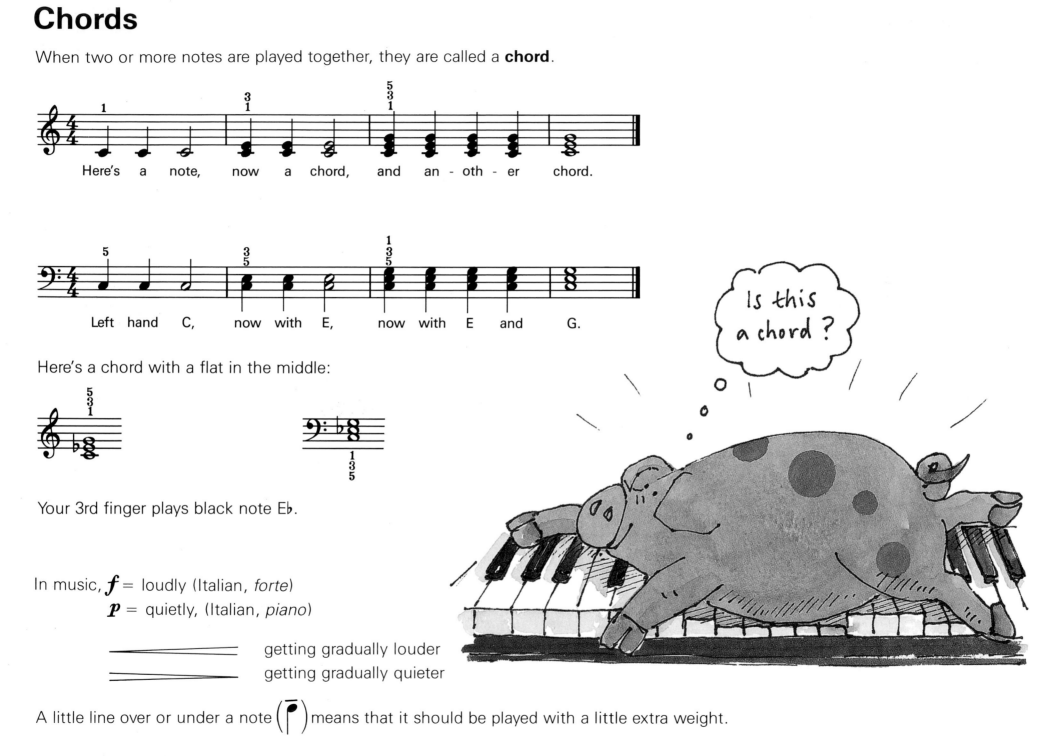

Here's a note, now a chord, and an-oth-er chord.

Left hand C, now with E, now with E and G.

Here's a chord with a flat in the middle:

Your 3rd finger plays black note E♭.

In music, **𝆑** = loudly (Italian, *forte*)

𝆏 = quietly, (Italian, *piano*)

getting gradually louder

getting gradually quieter

A little line over or under a note (𝅘𝅥) means that it should be played with a little extra weight.

Dinosaurs' Bedtime March

This tune has E♭s in it.

Before you play it, play these notes with your right and left hands:

Quite slowly

p ————————— *f*

What's that loud and fear-some roar? Can it be a di-no-saur?

Di - no-saurs with hea-vy tread March-ing up the stairs to bed.

p

(*zzzzz....!*)

New right-hand note: A

A

Do some jumps from G to A with your 5th finger.

Now try playing G with your 4th finger and A with your 5th.

It's much easier, isn't it?

Your thumb doesn't always play middle C.
In the next tune, your fingers are over different notes from the ones you have been used to.

Up the stairs I go to A, Now I'm sure I know the way.

Majestic March

Duet part

F   A

These two notes are both in spaces.

F is in the first space.

A is in the second space.

(Always count lines and spaces starting at the bottom, and going up.)

Spacemen

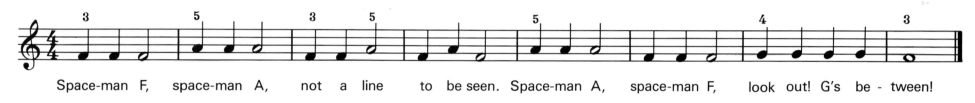

Space-man F,   space-man A,   not   a   line   to   be   seen.   Space-man A,   space-man F,   look   out!   G's   be - tween!

Lavender's Blue

In this tune you can play A by stretching your 5th finger up from G.

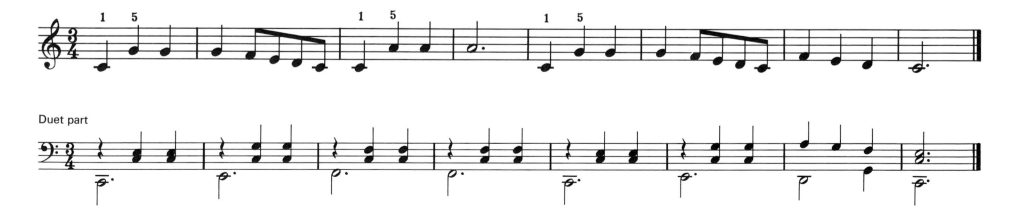

Duet part

Before you play *Camptown Races*, practise this clever little cross-over trick for your left-hand 2nd finger.

Look out for the places where it comes.

Camptown Races

Your left hand is the important one here. Play it a lot until you know the tune (your teacher will play the right hand part), then let your right hand have a go on its own. Later on you may find you can try your hands together, but GO SLOWLY!

Low C

Caribbean Carnival

Everyone is on holiday and having fun, so make this piece sound bright and cheerful. Look out for where your hand has to move up so that you can play A (in the middle bit).

Duet part

Daisy, Daisy

When your fingers know this piece, it needs to go quite quickly.

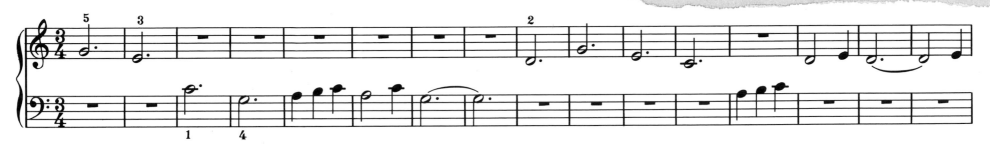

Duet part

Remember:

When a note is joined to another on the same line or space like this ♩ ♩ it is called a tied note. The second note isn't played again, just held on.

A page for your left hand

Do you remember your new left-hand notes?

Play them three times.
Now play these notes. Score 1 point for each.

SCORE

Write their names underneath them.

It's fun to play the bass part of a duet. Now's your chance! Not too loudly, or you won't be able to hear the tune in the treble.

Cowboy Song

Let your left hand practise on its own first.
Count steadily 1-2-3-4 in a bar.

Loud and soft

Can you play loudly (*f*) and softly (*p*)?
And can you make the music get gradually louder ⬤═══◁ or gradually softer ▷═══⬤ ?

Here's a piece for you to try.
 The bells are far away in the distance at first, but something happens to the sound as you get nearer....
(*pp* means very soft; *mf* means medium loud). Hold the right pedal down.

The Bells

Do you remember the other bell piece earlier in the book? Go back to page 14 and make sure you can still play it.
Making bell-sounds on the piano is fun — why not try inventing some of your own?

In these two tunes, your hands play together some of the time.
Don't let them play together until you have practised them on their own.

Oranges and Lemons

Old Dan Tucker

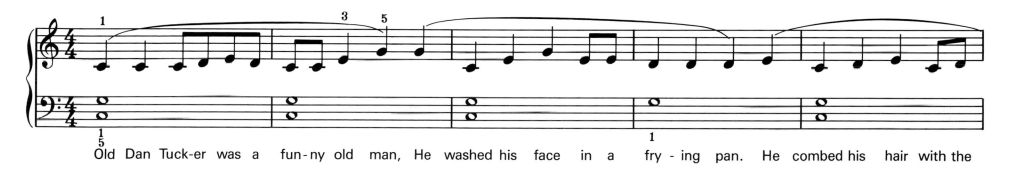

Old Dan Tuck-er was a fun-ny old man, He washed his face in a fry - ing pan. He combed his hair with the

leg of a chair, And all he said was, 'I DON'T CARE!'

Try playing the last three notes an octave lower—very loudly!

Three-hand Ragtime

Your left hand only plays four notes in this, and these four are played over and over again:
Your right hand doesn't do anything! Your teacher plays the top stave.

LOOK OUT! This bar is different...

THE END!

Are you ready for **PIANO TIME 1**? Before you go on to your next book, why not choose your three favourite pieces from this book, and give a concert to your friends? Practise them first to make sure that you can play them without any mistakes!